Pease Porridge Hot

Distributed by The Child's World®
1980 Lookout Drive • Mankato, MN 56003-1705
800-599-READ • www.childsworld.com

Acknowledgments
The Child's World®: Mary Berendes, Publishing Director
The Design Lab: Kathleen Petelinsek, Design

Library of Congress Cataloging-in-Publication Data
Billin-Frye, Paige.
 Pease porridge hot / illustrated by Paige Billin-Frye.
     p. cm.
 ISBN 978-1-60954-293-1 (library bound: alk. paper)
 1. Nursery rhymes. 2. Children's poetry. [1. Nursery rhymes.] I. Mother
Goose. II. Title.
 PZ8.3.B4945Pe 2011
 398.8—dc22
 [E]   2010032429

Printed in the United States of America in Mankato, Minnesota.
December 2010
PA02074

ILLUSTRATED BY PAIGE BILLIN-FRYE

Pease porridge hot.

Pease porridge cold.

Pease porridge in the pot,
nine days old.

Some like it hot.

Some like it cold.

Some like it in the pot,
nine days old.

SONG ACTIVITY

Pease porridge hot.

Pease porridge cold.

Pease porridge in the pot, nine days old.

Some like it hot.

Some like it cold.

Some like it in the pot, nine days old.

Two players face each other. When saying "pease," both players pat their hands on their own legs. On "porridge," both players clap their own hands together. When saying "hot," the players clap their hands against one another's.

Repeat the actions for "pease" and "porridge" again. When saying "cold," the players clap their hands against one another's again.

Repeat the actions for "pease" and "porridge" one more time. For the words "in the," the players clap their right hands together. On the word "pot," the players clap their own hands together. When saying "nine," the players clap their left hands together. On the word "days," the players clap their own hands together. On the word "old," the players clap their hands against one another's again.

BENEFITS OF NURSERY RHYMES AND ACTIVITY SONGS

Activity songs and nursery rhymes are more than just a fun way to pass the time. They are a rich source of intellectual, emotional, and physical development for a young child. Here are some of their benefits:

❀ Learning the words and activities builds the child's self-confidence—"I can do it all by myself!"

❀ The repetitious movements build coordination and motor skills.

❀ The close physical interaction between adult and child reinforces both physical and emotional bonding.

❀ In a context of "fun," the child learns the art of listening in order to learn.

❀ Learning the words expands the child's vocabulary. He or she learns the names of objects and actions that are both familiar and new.

❀ Repeating the words helps develop the child's memory.

❀ Learning the words is an important step toward learning to read.

❀ Reciting the words gives the child a grasp of English grammar and how it works. This enhances the development of language skills.

❀ The rhythms and rhyming patterns sharpen listening skills and teach the child how poetry works. Eventually the child learns to put together his or her own simple rhyming words— "I made a poem!"

ABOUT THE ILLUSTRATOR

Paige Billin-Frye studied illustration and design at Washington University in St. Louis Missouri, and graduated in 1981. Before she began illustrating children's books, Paige illustrated posters and magazine covers, and painted illustrations for greeting cards. Today, she works in a studio in the Takoma neighborhood of Washington, D.C., a few blocks from her house. Paige has illustrated more than thirty-five books for children.